STREETWISE
SELF DEFENCE
FOR WOMEN AND MEN

Edwin Deser

STREETWISE
SELF DEFENCE
FOR WOMEN AND MEN

W. FOULSHAM & CO. LTD.

London • New York • Toronto
Cape Town • Sydney

GV
7111
.D34
1989

W. FOULSHAM & COMPANY LIMITED

Yeovil Road, Slough, Berkshire, SL1 4JH

ISBN 0–572–01467–8

34519

Originally published by Falken-Verlag GmbH, Niedernhausen
TS. West Germany. © 1987. This English Language Edition Copyright © 1989
W. Foulsham & Co. Ltd.

*Whilst every effort has been made by
both the author and the publishers to
ensure that the contents of this book
have been carefully checked, no liability
can be accepted for personal injury or
material damage.*

Printed in Great Britain by
St Edmundsbury Press Ltd., Bury St Edmunds, Suffolk.

Contents

Introduction

This book has been written for those of us who do not want to take up the martial arts as a sport, but who would like to be able to defend ourselves in a potentially dangerous situation.

This course is intended to teach you to cope with practical situations, i.e. circumstances in which you may actually find yourself. You may not aspire to a black belt, but you will learn how to defend yourself effectively in an emergency.

You do not have to be particularly fit or well co-ordinated to use these techniques, which have also been designed for the not-so-strong. They are simple and easy to learn. They are also highly effective and suitable for both men and women.

Moves can be repeated in other defence actions, which means that the same moves can be adapted for use in different situations.

Unlike boxing, where flyweights are never matched against heavyweights, you should always assume that your attacker is stronger than you.

In an emergency, try to remember the following:

1 If at all possible, avoid a confrontation.
2 If you cannot avoid a fight, always kick or hit your attacker with as much force as you can.
3 Take the initiative and hit hard and fast.

'Practice makes perfect' they say, and this is true. Practise what you would do in a serious situation, so that you are sure of your moves. Try to do this with a partner, to help you practise the timing of these moves. Try to choose moves which you find easier and which come more naturally to you.

It is advisable to practise in your everyday clothes, as these are what you are most likely to be wearing in the event of an attack.

Some general ground rules

There are some important rules on how to react if attacked. If you bear these in mind, you already have the advantage over your attacker.

1 Breathe slowly and deeply to calm your nerves.
2 Always look your attacker in the eye.
3 Turn sideways to make it harder for your attacker to grab you.
4 Take up a defensive stance and stay as far away as possible.
5 Don't shout abuse – this may only antagonise your assailant.
6 Only use techniques you have really mastered. Don't hesitate, be decisive.
7 Avoid body holds.
8 Don't be afraid to kick and push.
9 Don't be heroic, get away to safety as quickly as you can.

Special rules for women

1 Turn and face your attacker so that you cannot be attacked from behind.
2 Run away screaming; make lots of noise if you think someone else will hear you.
3 If no one is nearby, then don't run. Engage your assailant in conversation. This way you gain time to calm yourself down and work out an effective strategy to fight off your attacker.
4 Try to improve your position. Look for the nearest house with lights, or a busy street.
5 Be careful not to let yourself be cornered, and don't allow yourself to be backed up into a doorway or against a wall.

The law and self defence

Section 3(1) of the Criminal Law Act 1967 states '. . .a person may use reasonable force in the prevention of crime . . .'

Obviously 'prevention of crime' covers a wide range, but this may include:

1 defence of yourself;
2 defence of another;
3 defence of property.

For the purposes of self defence, the following is true: in England (and Wales) what constitutes reasonable force is governed by common law. This means that you may use reasonable force to defend yourself from attack. What is considered 'reasonable' depends on the circumstances and is, ultimately, a matter for a jury to decide. Whether or not an attack has actually taken place will also be taken into account.

The degree of force used in self defence ought, in some way, to correspond to the nature of the attack. That is, if you have been slapped, it would be unreasonable to defend yourself with a knife. The test is one of reasonableness.

If you use more force than is reasonable in the circumstances, you could be prosecuted.

Formerly, self defence was permissible only as a last resort, for use if evasion and an attempt to retreat had failed.

This is no longer necessarily the law; you need not show reluctance to fight or attempt to retreat, but your actions must be reasonable in the circumstances. What is reasonable is a matter for a jury to decide in each individual case.

Shock tactics: the element of surprise

Surprise is an important factor in self defence. If used properly it throws your assailant off balance and may give you valuable time.

There are many types of shock tactics. We shall restrict ourselves to a few simple ones which will distract or confuse your attacker. This is an acquired defence tactic which could help you to save yourself.

Simple shock tactics:

- sudden, loud screaming;
- spitting in the attacker's face;
- throwing objects, such as bags, keys, papers or cigarette packets in the attacker's face;
- a powerful kick in the shins, or another sensitive part of the body.

The most vulnerable areas of the human body

The eyes and groin are your main targets. Direct your punches and kicks, as described, only at the marked points of the body, as otherwise they may not affect your attacker.

A hard kick or punch in the groin will quickly put men out of action, and can even render them unconscious. This is a very sensitive part of the body and very vulnerable to injury, no matter how big and strong a man may be.

You can achieve similar results by jabbing your assailant in the eyes with your fingers, which is one of the best methods of self defence. Your attacker will be helpless if he cannot see . . . and this applies equally to men and women. The simpler and more direct your counter attack, the more successful and effective you are likely to be.

Of course, the human body can be attacked in other areas which we have not described here. To prevent unnecessary confusion, we shall deal only with the most sensitive target areas.

In a life-threatening situation any self-defence methods used must be consistent and sustained until your assailant is disabled.

The practical advice given in this book will show you the various techniques to use and the way in which they can be adapted to any situation in which you may find yourself.

Main targets

Secondary targets

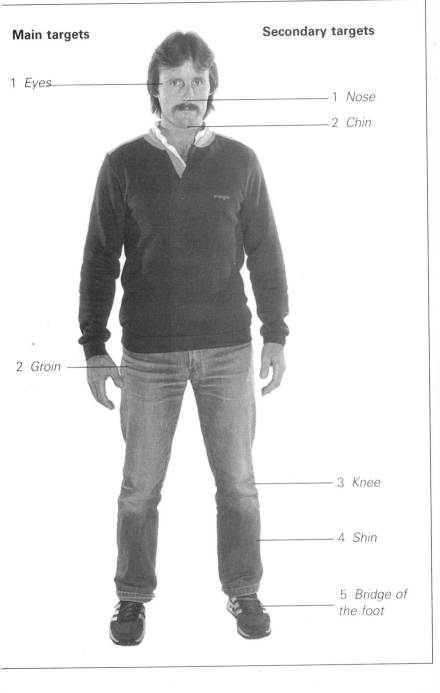

1 *Eyes*

1 *Nose*

2 *Chin*

2 *Groin*

3 *Knee*

4 *Shin*

5 *Bridge of the foot*

Practical training

The art of self defence can be learned by good practical training. This new system of self defence is based on the principle of versatility: in other words, one technique may be adapted to suit a variety of situations.

The book is divided into five chapters, the first three of which will teach you the basic techniques. This is why it is important to follow the sequence through in the correct order. It is a pointless exercise to attempt actual self-defence techniques without having first mastered the elementary hand, foot and blocking movements. The basic techniques must be practised so that you learn how to judge distances and how to develop just the right force of impact. Practise on a sack stuffed with old rags, to build up your confidence.

Once you have more or less mastered the basic tech-niques, you can turn to the chapter on attack and defence. Here, a partner is absolutely essential to give a more realistic 'feel' to your training. However, in practice sessions, certain restrictions apply, such as stopping just short of really hitting, punching or attacking your partner, to prevent injury. So remember – be careful!

It is a good idea to restrict yourself to practising only one type of attack per training session, such as body holds, for example. At the same time, keep practising the basic moves, so that these become second nature to you and you perform them smoothly.

This book also contains a chapter on using ordinary everyday items as weapons. You will learn how effectively you could defend yourself using a key, handbag, umbrella, book or even a newspaper.

The right stance

1 *Stance if you are right-handed*

2 *Stance if you are left-handed*

Correct stance is essential as a basis for all defence movements, and all the techniques can be performed from the stance shown in these pictures.

In order to achieve maximum mobility, balance your weight equally on both legs, keeping your knees slightly bent. Do not tense up; relax and be prepared to react quickly on all sides. Your shoulders should be diagonal to your assailant, so that you present the least surface area for your attacker to grab. Protect your chest and your chin by keeping your arms up at an angle. Clench your fists to minimise any damage to your fingers when defending or blocking.

This is not a static position, quite the opposite, and you should be constantly moving, like a boxer in the ring. Do not keep your arms still, but remember to keep up your guard.

This behaviour will confuse your attacker, leaving him no time to recognise the defensive action you may be taking. Try to stay out of reach of your attacker, but remember to maintain eye contact.

Using your fists

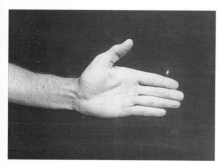

Making a fist in the correct way is very important to prevent any finger injuries when punching your assailant or using blocking techniques. These pictures show you how to clench a fist properly.

1 *Fingers outstretched*

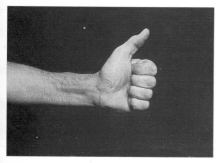

2 *Fingers bent in*

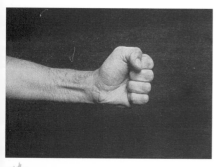

When your fist is clenched correctly, the thumb should lie in front of your index and middle finger, and *not* be covered by them.

3 *Correct clenching of fist*

Using your hands

This book will show you techniques in which you can use your hands, arms, elbows or fingers as weapons with which to disable your attacker.

The difference between a punch and a slap is the way in which the arm or hand movement is carried out. When pushing or punching, the arm movement is always straight ahead, towards the attacker, whereas, when slapping, the arm movement is circular or semi-circular (a swing or a hook).

In self defence it is very important to learn how to use your hands as weapons. A well-targeted punch, using the heel of your hand or elbow, is easily carried out and highly effective if your full body weight is behind it. Using these techniques, it is possible for a woman to floor a man who is physically stronger than her. The parts of the body to aim at have already been mentioned on page 12.

It is not necessary to harden the skin on your hands or elbows in order to make them less sensitive to pain; they have been designed by nature to resist knocks and punches. Amateurs can therefore use the various techniques without causing themselves injury.

Jabbing with the fingers is also very easy to learn and carry out and is also an extremely effective defence technique, which can stop an attack in the initial stages.

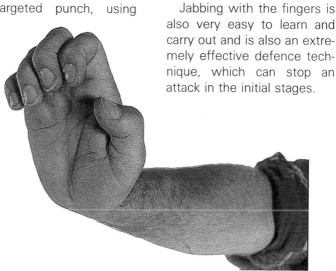

Good hand position

Jabbing with the heel of the hand

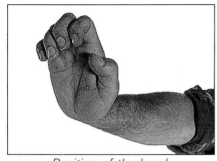

Bend the fingers up, hold your palm upright and bend it back as far back as you can.

Position of the hand

1 *2.* *3a*

PRACTICE

Take up the correct stance and push your hand forward with as much force as possible. The palm will connect with the target area. Remember to swivel your hips and follow through in the same direction.

The best effects can be achieved if you hit your attacker just under the nose.

Demonstration of jabbing with the heel of the hand

3b

1 *Your opponent is about to aim a punch at your head.*

3 *Block the punch and, at the same time, jab the heel of your hand under your attacker's nose.*

2 *Take evasive action by moving one step diagonally forward from the normal defence position.*

The finger jab

Close-up

This technique is highly effective but may also cause severe eye injuries. For this reason, the finger jab should only be used in life-threatening attacks. Never use unreasonable force, unless the situation you are in calls for it.

PRACTICE

Bend your index and middle fingers slightly. Stand in the correct basic stance and move forwards to carry out the finger jab.

1   *2*   *3*

Demonstration of the finger jab

1 *Your assailant is trying to strangle you with both hands.*

2 *Hunch your shoulders and pull your chin in to protect your neck.*

3 *Now jab your assailant in the eyes with your fingers, taking a step backwards at the same time.*

Elbowing your attacker

Close-up

Elbowing is very effective in close combat.

The most important thing to remember here is to bend your arm very sharply. You can elbow forwards or backwards. Your assailant is then hit by the area marked in the picture.

If you elbow forwards, your arm moves in a semi-circle, hitting the side of your attacker's face or his chin.

If you elbow backwards, stretch your arm out forwards, with the back of your clenched fist facing downwards, and then bring your arm backwards sharply and with as much force as you can muster.

In both cases, your fists should stay clenched and you should follow through with your shoulders.

Elbowing forwards

Elbowing backwards

Demonstration of the elbow punch

1 *Your attacker grabs your arm.*

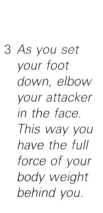

2 *You step forward, bringing your arm up in a semi-circle.*

3 *As you set your foot down, elbow your attacker in the face. This way you have the full force of your body weight behind you.*

Using your feet (kicking)

Using your legs gives you the advantage of greater reach, coupled with the fact that your legs are considerably stronger than your arms. If you react quickly enough, there is a good chance that you will be able to stop the attack in its initial stages. All the kicks are easy to learn if you follow the picture sequence. Good balance and speed are important. A quick, powerful kick to a sensitive part of the body (see page 13) is one of the best methods of self defence.

Aim your kicks below the belt and always kick with as much speed and force as possible.

One simple tried and tested method: kick your attacker in the knee and then get away to safety.

Kicking

Front kick

Close-up

PRACTICE

Start with your kicking foot behind you. Then raise your knee until your thigh is almost horizontal and kick sharply upwards with the lower half of your leg. Then bring your leg back quickly to the starting position, with your kicking foot behind you.

This kick is carried out in one movement, with the bridge of your foot hitting your attacker's groin. Imagine you are kicking a football with all your might.

1

2

3

Demonstration of the front kick

1 *The attacker grabs you with both arms.*

2 *You set your kicking foot behind you and spread your arms out.*

3 *Now lift your leg and shoot . . .*

4 *. . . your lower leg forwards.*

Side kick

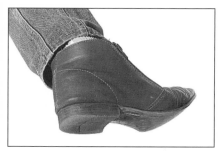

Close-up

This is an excellent kick for attack and defence, with the advantage that it cannot be blocked by your opponent.

1

2

PRACTICE

When you use the side kick, you hit either your attacker's knee or shin with the outside edge of your foot, or the sole of your foot.

Lift your front foot up to knee height and then, using your hip, kick sideways with as much force as you can, keeping your leg extended. By pivoting on your balancing foot, you will be able to use the full force of your hips and follow the movement through. If carried out correctly, the heel of your extended foot will point towards your assailant. Bring your leg back to the starting position immediately.

This technique is a sharp, powerful action backed by your full body weight.

To add power to your technique, lean a plank of wood against a wall and practise the hip movement, by kicking the plank until you can break it. Remember to keep your shoes on when practising this technique!

3

4

Side kick demonstration

1 *Your attacker grabs your arm.*

2 *Lift your front knee up.*

3 *Keeping your leg extended sideways, kick your attacker in the knee.*

4 *Then wrench your arm free.*

Heel stamp

Close-up

The heel stamp is used solely to distract your opponent, before you follow it up with another defence technique or action (for example, a jab with the heel of the hand).

1

2

PRACTICE

From your basic position, bring your knee up as high as possible and then stamp down sharply with the heel of your foot. As the close–up shows, your heel should hit the bridge of your assailant's foot. Remember to keep your toes pointing upwards, so that your heel is in the correct position.

If you are carrying out a heel stamp to the rear, keep your toes pointing down-wards, to make sure that you connect with your target.

3a

To the front

3b

To the rear

Demonstration of the heel stamp

1 *Your assailant grabs your arm.*

2 *Lift your foot . . .*

PRACTICE

Make sure that you always pull away in the direction of the weakest point, i.e. towards your attacker's little finger, rather than towards his thumb.

3 . . .and stamp on your assailant's foot with all your might.

4 Then wrench your arm free.

Kneeing your opponent

Close-up

This is a technique used in close combat and therefore ideally suited to self defence.

PRACTICE

Speed and power are essential for this move to be effective. The top of your knee should connect with your assailant's groin.

1   2

Demonstration

1 *Your assailant grabs you in a body hold with both arms.*

2 *Grab your assailant by the hips, push yourself away from him, at the same time stepping back with one leg.*

3 *Pull your opponent down and bring your knee up sharply into his groin, with as much force as you can.*

Blocking or defensive tactics

As you would expect, it is defence and not attack, which is the cornerstone of self defence. The object is to divert or deflect any blows or punches your assailant may be aiming at you, and to protect your own body from severe injury. It is only possible to attack your opponent if you first deflect his attack on you.

First, we should distinguish between the upward block, which deflects attacks to the head and shoulders, and the downward block, which prevents attacks on the chest and abdomen.

The blocking or defensive techniques shown here can be used to deflect such attacks.

When defending yourself, never carry out only a blocking movement, without following it up with a counter move. Only by doing both, will you be able to prevent any renewed attack, and also protect yourself.

Blocking technique

Upward block

Close-up

Block the attacking arm with the area of the forearm shown in the close–up.

PRACTICE

Move your rear leg diagonally forward from the basic stance, bringing your arm up in front of your face. The power of any attack on you can be further 'diluted' by stepping to the side or rear with the other leg.

1   2   3

Demonstration of the upward block

1 *You are in the basic defence stance.*

2 *Your attacker tries to throw a punch to your head. You move diagonally forwards, deflecting the power of the blow.*

3 *The underside of your forearm immediately blocks your attacker's striking arm.*

Downward block

1 2 3

PRACTICE

Here, again, you should move diagonally forward from the basic position and bring your arm down to protect the lower part of your body.

Demonstration of the downward block

1 *Your assailant attempts to punch you in the abdomen.*

2 *From the basic stance, move diagonally forward, slamming your arm down sharply on your opponent's wrist.*

3 *Now deflect your assailant's striking arm to the side, weakening the potential force of the blow.*

Attack and defence

This chapter deals with a number of different dangerous situations which you may be unlucky enough to encounter. With a little practice, you will be able to develop the right instinctive techniques for effective self defence. It is absolutely vital to life and limb to keep a cool head and to think your strategy through calmly.

Blocking, striking and running away are the three most important elements in self defence. Learn to master the techniques step by step, so that, in any potentially dangerous situation, you will be fully in control of yourself. Keep the following in mind:

1 Practise punching, kicking and jabbing as described in the first chapters of this book, but very slowly at first.
2 When you have mastered the moves slowly, build up your speed and power, but without a partner (you may find it helpful to practise in front of a mirror).
3 Finally, practise your self defence techniques with a partner, so that you can put what you have learned into practice and get used to body contact.

Defensive movement

Defence against grabbing and holding

Wrenching free from a body hold is not always easy. This is why it is crucial to react as quickly as possible if an assailant tries to grab and hold you, so that the attack can be stopped in its initial stages. However, if your attacker has already managed to get you in a body hold, the next few pages should help you to deal with this. By using the following techniques, with as much power as you can, you will probably be able to break free.

1 *Your attacker (on the right) tries to grab you.*

2 *A powerful kick in the groin will disable your attacker before he has a chance to take hold of you.*

FINGER WRENCH

This can be extremely painful if properly carried out. The pain can be maximised by pulling and twisting the finger joints. Pull the fingers away from the joints: in the case shown in the picture this is up and back across the back of the hand. Pull the little finger if possible, as this is the weakest joint.

Finger wrench for dealing with a rear body hold

Finger wrench for dealing with a double Nelson

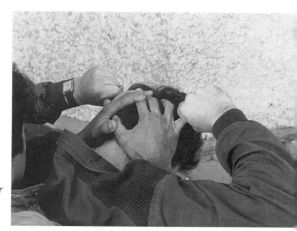

COMPRESSION BLOW

Cup your hands over your assailant's ears, as shown in the picture, and then slam your hands very sharply into the side of the head, so that the compressed air in your hands creates pressure in the ears of your adversary. This creates a balance disturbance and temporarily disables your attacker.

Compression blow

HEAD BUTT

Use your forehead, or the back of your head, to butt your opponent. This move has the advantage of the element of surprise and will not injure you, providing you hit your attacker's nose. You will be considerably more sure of hitting home if you can grip your attacker's head.

Head butt to the front

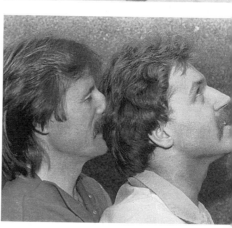

Head butt to the rear

Getting out of a one-arm hold

1 *You are leaning against a fence.*

2 *A man tries to force his attentions on you, placing an arm around your shoulders.*

3 *Elbow him sharply in the ribs . . .*

4 *. . . and follow up with a powerful punch to the nose.*

Dealing with an ambush

1 *You are walking along the street.*

2 *Suddenly someone grabs you and tries to force his attentions on you.*

3 *Raise your knee . . .*

4 *. . . and, using the front kick technique, kick your assailant in the groin.*

Dealing with a shoulder hold from behind

1 *A man is following you.*

2 *He grabs you by the shoulder and tries to pull you towards him.*

3 *Spin round as fast as you can . . .*

4 *. . . and jab his nose with the heel of your hand.*

Defending yourself whilst seated

1 *You are sitting on a bench.*

2 *A man sits down next to you and puts his hand on your knee.*

3 *Stay seated, swivel round and jab him in the nose with the heel of your hand.*

When your bag is grabbed from behind

1 *You are standing in the street.*

2 *Suddenly someone grabs your bag from behind.*

3 *Bend your arm inwards to hold on tight to your bag.*

4 *And follow up with a side kick to the knee.*

If your hair is pulled from the side

1 *An assailant approaches from behind.*

2 *And then pulls your hair from the side.*

3 *Grab your opponent's arm and turn inwards to face him.*

4 *Then jab your attacker on the nose with the heel of your hand.*

If your hair is pulled from the front

1 *Your assailant pulls your hair from the front.*

2 *Grab him by the hips . . .*

3 *. . . pull him down and slam your knee into his groin.*

Dealing with a diagonal hand hold

1 *Your assailant grabs you by the forearm.*

2 *Step towards your assailant.*

3 *Jab him in the nose with the heel of your hand . . .*

4 *. . . and wrench your arm away.*

If you are attacked getting out of your car

1 *Your attacker opens your car door . . .*

2 *. . . and tries to pull you out of the car.*

3 *Lean back across the passenger seat . . .*

4 *. . . and slam your heel into your opponent's face or groin.*

If you do not have time to carry out the above move, you may still be able to defend yourself with a finger jab to the eyes.

Defence against body holds
Underarm hold from behind

1 *You are about to open your car door.*

2 *At that moment you are grabbed from the rear.*

3 *You raise your knee . . .*

4 . . . and stamp hard on your opponent's foot.

5 Then grab your assailant's little finger and pull it right back. Your assailant will loosen his grip and you will be able to break free.

6 Then jab his nose with the heel of your hand.

Overarm hold from behind

1 *Your attacker grabs you from behind with both arms.*

2 *Raise your knee . . .*

3 *. . . and stamp hard on your assailant's foot.*

4 *Now pull your arm forward . . .*

5 *. . . and snap it back sharply into your assailant's ribs.*

6 *Turn to face your attacker and jab him in the nose with the heel of your hand.*

Getting out of a double Nelson

1 *Your opponent has got you in a double Nelson.*

2 *You react with the utmost speed and raise your knee.*

3 *Stamp with all your weight, keeping your heel well down.*

4 *Then move your arms up and pull your attacker's little finger . . .*

5 *. . . wrenching it to the side.*

6 *Once you have broken free, slam your elbow back into your attacker.*

Underarm hold from the front

1 *You are walking along a path.*

2 *Suddenly you are grabbed from the front by someone walking towards you.*

3 *Hit your attacker on both ears using a compression blow . . .*

4 *. . . and break free, jabbing your assailant's nose with the heel of your hand.*

Overarm body hold from the front

1 *Your opponent grabs you with both arms.*

2 *Raise your knee . . .*

3 *. . . and stamp hard on your attacker's foot so that he will loosen his grip.*

4 *Then knee your assailant in the groin.*

Getting out of a head hold

1 *Your attacker has your head in a firm hold.*

2 *Hit your attacker in the groin with the heel of your hand.*

3 *At the same time, use your other hand to pull your attacker's hair . . .*

4 *. . . and pull him backwards away from you.*

5 *Then jab your attacker on the chin with the heel of your hand.*

Defence against strangle holds
Strangle holds from behind

1 *Your assailant approaches from behind*

2 *. . . and begins to strangle you.*

3 *Tense your neck muscles and stretch your arms out in front . . .*

4 . . . and then elbow your assailant in the ribs, as hard as you can. At the same time, use your other hand to free yourself from the strangle hold.

5 Then turn around and jab your attacker's nose with the heel of your hand.

Strangle holds from the front

1 *You are just about to get into your car.*

2 *You are attacked and your assailant tries to strangle you with both hands.*

3 *From the basic position, jab your assailant in the nose with the heel of your hand, following through with your hips to help you hit with more strength.*

4 *If this does not work, use a finger jab to help you break free.*

Forearm strangle holds from behind

1 *You are sitting down when you are grabbed from behind.*

2 *Tense your neck muscles immediately . . .*

3 *. . . and pull your attacker's hair forwards.*

4 *If your attacker's grip becomes too tight, use a finger jab.*

If you are attacked in the car

1 *The attacker tries to strangle you through the car window.*

2 *Tense your neck muscles . . .*

3 *. . . and finger jab your attacker in the eyes.*

If you are thrown to the ground

1 *Your attacker tries to strangle you after having thrown you to the ground.*

2 *Jab him in the eyes with your fingers.*

3 *Then pull your assailant's hair with one hand and take hold of his chin with the other.*

4 *Pull your attacker's head downwards, twisting it at the same time, using your other hand (neck twist). Pull your leg up and roll over sideways, freeing yourself from your attacker.*

Techniques to use if thrown to the ground

1 *Your assailant has brought you down and is approaching you again.*

2 *He is about to kick you. Raise your knee . . .*

Note: *if attacked when lying down, make sure your legs and feet are facing your assailant, as this gives him the least possible opportunity to grab you.*

3 *. . . and then kick your opponent on the shin, using the side kick technique.*

Defence against fist attacks
Fist punch from behind

1 *You are leaning over the boot of the car. Your assailant . . .*

2 *. . . grabs hold of your right shoulder and tries to throw a right-hand punch to your head.*

3 *Turn round to face your attacker and block the punch with your left arm . . .*

4 *. . . then jab your assailant's nose with the heel of your hand.*

Fist punch from the front

1 *You are about to open the door of a telephone box.*

2 *Without warning someone tries to punch you.*

3 *You block the punch and . . .*

4 *. . . jab your assailant's nose with the heel of your hand.*

If punched when sitting

1 *Your attacker approaches you while you are sitting down . . .*

2 *. . . and tries to punch you. Turn sideways away from your attacker . . .*

3 . . . and block the punch
with your forearm . . .

4 . . . then jab your attacker
in the groin with the heel
of your hand. Your fingers
should be pointing
towards the ground.

If grabbed by the lapel

1 *Your attacker grabs hold of your lapel with his left hand and tries to punch you with his right.*

2 *You take evasive action to the right, blocking the punch at the same time.*

3 *Slam your left knee into your attacker's groin . . .*

4 *. . . and then jab your attacker's ear with the heel of your hand.*

Defence against weapon attacks

How to defend yourself if you are threatened with a weapon is one of the most difficult chapters in this book. If you have not fully mastered the techniques, your situation is a hazardous one. The best advice is to try to avoid this type of confrontation in the first place. If this is not possible, be as determined as you can and do not show any hesitation.

Defending yourself against a weapon

If threatened with a gun

Try to lull your attacker into a sense of security. Show that you are frightened and distract your assailant by trying to engage him in conversation. Any offensive action you may take has to start with a diversion. One old, but surprisingly effective, ruse is to look over your assailant's shoulder, for example, and act as if you have seen something important or surprising. Do not make a move until your assailant has fallen for the trick. The element of surprise is very important, so you must act with the utmost speed.

1 *Your assailant is holding a gun to your chest.*

2 *After you have distracted your attacker, take evasive action sideways, grab the assailant's gun hand and push it away from you. Then, if the gun should go off, the bullet will not hit you.*

  Keep hold of the attacker's hand until he has let go of the gun.

3 *After taking evasive action – always keep the assailant's gun hand blocked – jab your attacker in the eyes with your fingers.*

4 *Hold the assailant's gun hand with one hand and grab hold of the gun from the outside with the other.*

5 *Now wrench the gun free and pull it away backwards. You must always disarm your opponent in order to prevent a further attack.*

If threatened with a stick

If you are threatened with a stick, make sure you dodge out of your attacker's way, then come in as close as pos-sible, leaving him no room to raise the stick or put any power into a blow.

1 *Your opponent is facing you, armed with a stick: he tries to hit you.*

2 *From the basic stance, take one step sideways and reach up to block the blow, thus deflecting its force.*

3 *After this evasive action, jab your assailant in the eyes with your fingers.*

4 *Now grab the stick and pull it downwards out of your assailant's hand.*

If threatened with a knife

This is a very dangerous situation. Again, try to distract or disable your attacker, by throwing keys in his face for example.

1 *Stand in the basic position.*

2 *Your opponent tries to stab you. You block his arm and take a step diagonally forward at the same time . . .*

3 . . . then lean forward and jab your opponent in the eyes with your fingers.

4 Keep hold of your assailant's arm until you have removed the weapon.

Everyday articles as weapons

This chapter shows how everyday articles can become weapons.

Umbrellas, keys, books, newspapers and other objects, which you may be carrying, can be used in self defence. Any sprays, such as deodorant, hairspray or perfume can also be extremely useful, as you can spray this into your attacker's eyes.

Women may also defend themselves with high heeled shoes, by taking them off and using them to hit an assailant in the face or groin.

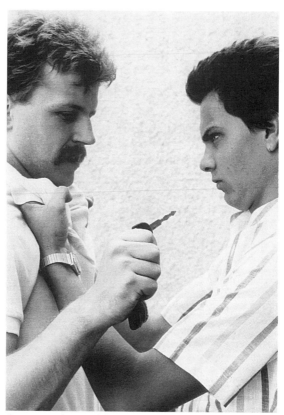

An everyday article as a weapon

Using a key

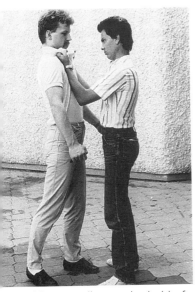

1 Your assailant grabs hold of your collar with both hands.

2 With a key in your hand . . .

3 . . . stab your assailant in the side of the face.

4 Follow this up by jabbing your assailant's nose with the heel of your hand to free yourself completely.

Using a rolled-up newspaper

1 *Your attacker grabs your arm from behind.*

2 *Turn and face your attacker . . .*

3 *. . . and jab him under the nose with the rolled-up newspaper.*

Using a book against an attack from the front

1 *Your attacker grabs you from the front . . .*

2 *. . . and prepares to punch you. You step forward and block the punch with your forearm . . .*

3 *. . . and jab the book under your assailant's nose*

Using a book against an attack from the side

1 *Your attacker approaches from the side . . .*

2 *. . . and grabs your shoulder.*

3 *You turn away sideways . . .*

4 *. . . and jab the book under your assailant's nose with both hands.*

Using an umbrella

1 *You are strolling along the street.*

2 *Your attacker grabs you from behind and tries to force his attentions upon you.*

3 *You immediately swivel your hips away . . .*

4 *. . . and slam your umbrella into your assailant's groin.*

Using a handbag

1 *You are walking along in the park.*

2 *Your assailant pesters you and tries to stop you.*

3 *Without hesitating, you take your handbag from your shoulder and hit your attacker in the face with it, distracting him for a moment.*

4 *Then you can use a front kick to kick your assailant in the groin.*